Recipes by Catherine Quévremont

Tart Tatins

Photographs by Deirdre Rooney

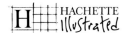

sweet recipes

savoury recipes

tips and tricks

First, a quick explanation of how the tart Tatin got its name. The Tatin sisters ran an inn at Lamotte-Beuvron in France. One day, the more absent-minded of the two sisters forgot to put the pastry base for the apple pie in the bottom of the baking tin before adding the filling; having no alternative she simply put it on top.

If considered from a more technical point of view, however, the interesting aspect of this French equivalent of an 'upside-down cake' is that the filling is cooked beneath a layer of pastry, which prevents it from drying out in the oven. The pastry lid retains a greater degree of humidity, and as a result the filling is almost steamed, which makes for interesting flavour combinations.

Which baking tin should I use?

A tin with a non-stick coating is best, because the tart will be easier to turn out, even if the filling has caramelized.

A fixed-based baking tin is essential to prevent the cooking juices from running out of the tin.

Before it is cooked, a tart Tatin is quite deep; the filling collapses slightly as it cooks. For this reason, it's best to use a deep rather than a shallow baking tin.

Many different sorts of baking dish are suitable for making tart Tatins:

• Individual ramekin dishes

• A soufflé dish

• A square, round or oval ovenproof dish

• Even a cast-iron frying pan: use it first to caramelize the fruit, then top with a pre-cooked round of pastry.

Tart pastries

A sweet shortcrust pastry is the traditional choice for making a fruit tart Tatin, but there is nothing to stop you using other types.

Puff pastry is better for fruits that produce a lot of water during cooking. Buy frozen or chilled ready-made puff pastry and follow maker's instructions for use.

Another alternative is to rub sweet pastry dough with the fingertips until it resembles breadcrumbs, as for a crumble. Pat the mixture down firmly so as to make a solid crust base when you turn out the tart.

Alternative suggestions

• Cut a disc of sponge cake to fit the baking tin and place over an almond-and-fruit cream filling.

• Cut two buckwheat pancakes to fit the baking tin, then brush with butter so that they become crisp when cooked, and place over a fish or shellfish filling.

a selection of suitable pastries

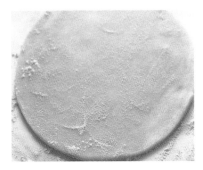

Shortcrust pastry

250 g (8 oz) plain flour

pinch of salt

125 g (4 oz) butter, softened

water

Sift the flour and salt together in a mixing bowl. Make a well in the centre, add the butter and rub in with the fingertips until the mixture resembles large breadcrumbs.

Add a little water and knead to form a soft dough, adding more water if necessary. Leave to rest in the refrigerator for 1 hour before using.

Sweet pastry

250 g (8 oz) plain flour

125 g (4 oz) caster sugar

pinch of salt

150 g (5 oz) unsalted butter, very soft

1 egg, beaten

water

Sift the flour, sugar and salt together in a mixing bowl. Make a well in the

centre and add the butter. Rub in with the fingertips, working quickly so that the dough does not turn into breadcrumbs. Add the egg and a little water, and knead lightly to form a soft dough, adding more water if necessary. Leave to rest in the refrigerator for 1 hour before using the pastry.

Cornflake pastry

200 g (7 oz) cornflakes

150 g (5 oz) unsalted butter

warm milk

½ sachet dried yeast

4 tablespoons cornflour

1 tablespoon caster sugar

Crush the cornflakes coarsely using a rolling pin, then transfer to a large mixing bowl.

Soften the butter in a microwave oven, then combine with the milk and yeast.

Add the cornflour, sugar, milk and melted butter to the crushed cornflakes and combine to produce a soft dough.

Parmesan pastry

200 g (7 oz) plain flour

1 teaspoon table salt

100 g (3½ oz) Parmesan cheese, grated

50 g (2 oz) Gruyère cheese, grated

½ sachet dried yeast

2 eggs

1 teacup milk

2–3 tablespoons mustard

125 g (4 oz) unsalted butter, melted

Sift the flour and salt together and add the Parmesan, Gruyère and yeast. Beat the eggs together with the milk and add to the flour mixture. Knead to form a smooth dough, then stir in the mustard, followed by the melted butter.

Apple Tatin

Serves 6

5 apples: Golden Russet, Braeburn, or Cox's Orange Pippin

100 g (3½ oz) butter

3 tablespoons sugar

½ teaspoon vanilla essence

250 g (8 oz) shortcrust pastry (see page 5)

Preheat the oven to 200°C (400°F), gas mark 6.

Peel and core the apples, then cut them into slices 2-cm (³/₄-inch) thick.

Melt the butter in a frying pan and fry the apple slices for 1–2 minutes on each side until golden.

Sprinkle the sugar over the base of a baking tin, arrange the apple slices evenly on top, and sprinkle with the vanilla essence. Top with the rolled-out pastry, making a small hole in the centre to allow the steam to escape.

Bake for 10 minutes, then reduce heat to 110°C (225°F), gas mark ¼ and bake for a further 20 minutes.

Remove from the oven and immediately turn the tart out onto a serving dish. Serve with crème fraîche, whipped cream or a scoop of vanilla ice cream.

Apricot Tatin

Serves 6

12 firm fresh apricots

50 g (2 oz) unsalted butter

1 tablespoon olive oil

2 egg yolks

50 g (2 oz) sugar

150 ml (¼ pint) crème fraîche

25 g (1 oz) pine nuts, toasted

250 g (8 oz) ready-made puff pastry

Preheat the oven to 110°C (225°F), gas mark ¼.

Halve the apricots and remove the stones. Heat the butter and oil in a non-stick frying pan and fry the apricot halves for 2 minutes on each side until golden. They should remain firm. Place on kitchen paper to drain.

Meanwhile, beat the egg yolks together with the sugar and the crème fraîche.

Arrange the apricot halves in the base of a baking tin, cut sides up, sprinkle with the pine nuts and pour over the crème fraîche mixture. Top with the rolled-out pastry, pressing down firmly to seal at the sides of the baking tin.

Bake for 10 minutes, then increase the heat to 180°C (350°F), gas mark 4 and bake for a further 20 minutes.

Pear Tatin

Serves 6

50 g (2 oz) sugar

1 vanilla pod, split in half

3 Comice pears

50 g (2 oz) raisins

2 tablespoons rum

3 eggs

2 tablespoons ground almonds

250 g (8 oz) shortcrust pastry (see page 5)

In a large pan, heat 1 litre (1¾ pints) water with the sugar and the vanilla pod until the sugar has melted. Peel and halve the pears, remove the core, place the halves in the sugar syrup and cook for 10 minutes. Remove the pears with a slotted spoon and leave to drain on a wire rack. Reserve the syrup.

Place the raisins in a bowl, sprinkle with 1 tablespoon of the rum and 2 tablespoons of the reserved pear syrup. Leave to soak for 30 minutes.

Preheat the oven to 180°C (350°F), gas mark 4.

Beat the eggs together with the ground almonds and the remaining rum.

Arrange the pears cut sides up in the base of a baking tin scatter over the raisins and cover with the almond mixture. Top with the rolled-out pastry and bake for 25 minutes.

Rhubarb Tatin

Serves 6

750 g (1 ½ lb) rhubarb

3 slices gingerbread

75 g (3 oz) soft brown sugar

2 tablespoons Irish whiskey

250 g (8 oz) shortcrust
pastry (see page 5)

Preheat the oven to 180°C (350°F), gas mark 4.

Cut the rhubarb into chunks about 2 cm (¾ inch) thick.

Crumble the slices of gingerbread. Sprinkle the brown sugar over the base of a baking tin, then add the first layer of rhubarb and sprinkle with half the crumbled gingerbread and 1 tablespoon whiskey. Add a second layer of rhubarb, then scatter with the remaining gingerbread and whiskey.

Top with the rolled-out pastry, tucking the pastry down well inside the baking tin. Bake for 45 minutes.

Serve with custard flavoured with whiskey.

Orange Tatin

Serves 6

3 unwaxed or well-scrubbed
oranges

250 ml (8 fl oz) golden syrup

250 g (8 oz) mascarpone

2 eggs

2 tablespoons Cointreau

250 g (8 oz) ready-made
puff pastry

Remove the rind of one of the oranges with a zester or sharp knife and blanch for 2 minutes in boiling water. Heat the golden syrup, add the blanched zest and caramelize for 10 minutes. Remove the zest with a slotted spoon and drain, reserving 1 tablespoon of the caramelized syrup.

Preheat the oven to 200°C (400°F), gas mark 6.

Remove the peel and pith from all the oranges. Using a sharp knife, cut the oranges into quarters. Cut between each segment, but stop before you get to the centre. Place the orange quarters to drain on kitchen paper.

In a bowl, combine the mascarpone with the eggs, caramelized syrup, orange zest and liqueur, stirring well.

Arrange the orange quarters over the base of a baking tin, pour over the mascarpone mixture, then top with the rolled-out puff pastry, sealing the pastry edges well by pinching them against the sides of the baking tin.

Bake for 10 minutes, then reduce heat to 160°C (325°F), gas mark 3 and bake for a further 20 minutes.

Peach Tatin

Serves 6

5 white peaches

200 g (7 oz) redcurrants

50 g (2 oz) unsalted butter

50 g (2 oz) soft brown sugar

50 g (2 oz) blanched almonds

250 g (8 oz) shortcrust pastry (see page 5)

Skin and halve the peaches, remove the stones, and leave to drain on a wire rack or kitchen paper.

Preheat the oven to 200°C (400°F), gas mark 6.

Remove the stalks from the redcurrants. Melt the butter in a frying pan and quickly fry the redcurrants over a high heat, stirring constantly with a wooden spoon, for 7–8 minutes. Using the back of the spoon, crush any berries that have not collapsed during cooking.

Pass the crushed redcurrants through a fine sieve. If the juice is too runny, return it to the frying pan and boil vigorously until it thickens. It should coat the back of a spoon.

Sprinkle the brown sugar over the base of a baking tin, add the almonds, pour over the redcurrant juice and arrange the peach halves evenly.

Top with the rolled-out pastry, taking care to seal it well to the sides of the baking tin. Bake for 25 minutes.

Mango Tatin

Serves 6

2 large (or 3 medium), ripe mangoes

3 passion fruit

50 g (2 oz) unsalted butter

50 g (2 oz) soft brown sugar

2 tablespoons white rum

2 allspice berries

250 g (8 oz) shortcrust pastry (see page 5)

Peel the mangoes and cut into thick slices, reserving any juice that is produced.

Preheat the oven to 200°C (400°F), gas mark 6.

Cut open the passion fruit and pass the flesh through a fine sieve to remove the pips. Melt the butter and sugar in a large saucepan. Add the mango and passion fruit juices and the rum. Boil for 10 minutes until very thick.

Pour the caramelized juice into a baking tin, and arrange the mango slices on top. Crush the allspice berries and sprinkle over the mangoes. Top with the rolled-out pastry, taking care to seal it firmly at the edges, and bake for 25 minutes.

Cherries in brandy Tatin

Serves 6

500 g (1 lb) fresh black cherries

500 g (1 lb) cherries in brandy

½ jar, about 170 g (6 oz) cherry jam

250 g (8 oz) shortcrust pastry (see page 5)

Remove the stones from the fresh cherries, reserving any juice. Also remove the stones from the cherries in brandy, reserving 3 tablespoons of the brandy.

Preheat the oven to 200°C (400°F), gas mark 6.

Put all the cherries and jam in a large pan, together with the juice collected from the fresh cherries and the reserved juice from the cherries in brandy, and boil vigorously to produce a thick compote.

Spread the cherry compote over the base of a baking tin. For even more flavour, scatter over a few whole cherries in brandy. Top with the rolled-out pastry, taking care to seal it firmly at the edges, and bake for 25 minutes.

Prune Tatin

Serves 6

1 Earl Grey teabag

400 g (13 oz) prunes, pitted

150 ml (¼ pint) Armagnac (or Cognac)

2 tablespoons soft brown sugar

2 large fresh black figs

250 g (8 oz) ready-made puff pastry

Put the teabag in a medium-sized heatproof bowl and pour over 250 ml (8 fl oz) boiling water and leave to infuse. Add the prunes to the tea, together with the Armagnac or Cognac, and leave to soak overnight, or for at least 6 hours.

Preheat the oven to 220°C (425°F), gas mark 7.

Lift out the prunes with a slotted spoon and put in a large saucepan together with 4 tablespoons of the soaking juices. Add the sugar and boil, stirring, for 10 minutes or until the prunes have softened to form a compote.

Cut the figs into quarters, arrange over the base of a baking tin, cut side facing downwards, and cover with the prune compote. Top with the rolled-out pastry, seal well at the sides of the baking tin, and bake for 25 minutes.

Quince Tatin

Serves 6

3 large quince

4 tablespoons lemon juice

75 g (3 oz) salted butter

2 tablespoons chestnut honey, or other well-flavoured honey

a few pinches of cinnamon

250 g (8 oz) shortcrust pastry (see page 5)

Peel the quince, cut into thick slices and sprinkle with the lemon juice to prevent them from discolouring.

Preheat the oven to 200°C (400°F), gas mark 6.

Melt the butter and honey in a deep-sided frying pan. Add the sliced quince and brown in the butter for 10 minutes, turning frequently. Remove the quince with a slotted spoon and then boil the cooking juices until they have reduced to form a caramel sauce.

Arrange the caramelized quince slices in the base of a baking tin, sprinkle with the cinnamon and pour over the caramel sauce.

Top with the rolled-out pastry, seal well at the edges and bake for 25 minutes.

Banana and chocolate Tatin

Serves 6

4 bananas

4 tablespoons lemon juice

50 g (2 oz) unsalted butter

50 g (2 oz) sugar

1 teaspoon vanilla essence

100-g (3½-oz) packet plain cooking chocolate drops

250 g (8 oz) shortcrust pastry (see page 5)

Preheat the oven to 180°C (350°F), gas mark 4.

Peel and slice the bananas, then sprinkle with the lemon juice to prevent them from discolouring.

Melt the butter, sugar and vanilla essence in a large frying pan, then carefully fry the banana slices until golden, taking care that they do not disintegrate.

Arrange the chocolate drops evenly over the base of a baking tin, cover with two layers of sliced banana, then top with the rolled-out pastry and bake for 25 minutes.

Delicious served with a scoop of chocolate ice cream.

Pineapple and kiwifruit Tatin

Serves 6

6 slices fresh pineapple

3 egg yolks

3 tablespoons grated coconut

50 g (2 oz) sugar

200 ml (7 fl oz) crème fraîche

250 g (8 oz) shortcrust pastry (see page 5)

3 kiwifruit

Preheat the oven to 160°C (325°F), gas mark 3.

Arrange the pineapple slices on a baking sheet and bake in the oven for 10 minutes until they have dried out slightly.

Beat the egg yolks together with the coconut, sugar and crème fraîche.

Remove the pineapple slices from the oven and cut into quarters. Arrange the pineapple pieces over the base of a non-stick baking tin, cover with the coconut and crème fraîche mixture and top with the rolled-out pastry.

Bake for 25 minutes. When cooked, remove from the oven and leave to cool for 10 minutes before turning out.

Peel the kiwifruit, cut into very thin slices and arrange over the tart. It is best not to cook the kiwifruit.

Bilberry Tatin

Serves 6

4 tablespoons water

100 g (3½ oz) sugar

500 g (1 lb) bilberries,
or blueberries

2 leaves gelatine (see note)

250 g (8 oz) shortcrust
pastry (see page 5)

Preheat the oven to 180°C (350°F), gas mark 4.

Heat the water and sugar in a saucepan to form a light syrup. Add the bilberries and simmer gently for 10 minutes.

Soften the gelatine leaves in cold water, then squeeze to expel the water. Add the gelatine to the bilberries while they are still cooking and stir well to dissolve.

Pour the bilberry mixture into a baking tin, top with the rolled-out pastry, and bake for 25 minutes. Leave to cool for 10 minutes before turning out.

Note: If leaf gelatine is not readily available, as an alternative you can use 1½ teaspoons powdered gelatine following the maker's instructions.

Tomato and sardine Tatin

Serves 6

12 fresh sardine fillets

1 kg (2 lb) tomatoes

2 tablespoons olive oil

sprig of rosemary

250 g (8 oz) ready-made puff pastry

large knob of butter, melted

sea salt and freshly ground black pepper

Preheat the oven to its lowest setting.

Carefully wipe the sardine fillets, making sure you remove any remaining bones.

Halve the tomatoes and place them, cut side up, on a baking sheet. Drizzle with olive oil, season with salt and place a few rosemary leaves on each tomato. Bake for 20 minutes, then remove from the oven.

Increase the oven temperature to 200°C (400°F), gas mark 6.

Arrange the sardine fillets evenly over the lightly oiled base of a baking tin, cover with the baked tomatoes and top with the rolled-out pastry.

Brush the pastry with the melted butter and bake for 25 minutes.

Turn the tart out onto a serving dish, season with sea salt and freshly ground black pepper and drizzle with a little olive oil if necessary.

Tomato and mozzarella Tatin

Serves 6

2 x 400-g (14-oz) cans
peeled whole tomatoes

1 garlic clove, peeled

bunch of basil, washed

1 tablespoon olive oil

1 x 125 g (4½ oz) buffalo
milk mozzarella cheese
(*mozzarella di bufala*)

250 g (8 oz) ready-made
puff pastry

sea salt and freshly ground
black pepper

few sprigs fresh oregano,
to garnish

Drain, deseed and coarsely chop the tomatoes. Chop the peeled garlic and washed basil.

Preheat the oven to 200°C (400°F), gas mark 6.

Heat the oil in a large frying pan and fry the tomatoes sprinkled with the garlic and basil and seasoned with salt and pepper. Cook over a high heat until the mixture is almost dry.

Drain the mozzarella cheese, pat dry with kitchen paper and cut into thick slices.

Place the cheese slices over the base of a baking tin, pour over the tomato sauce and top with the rolled-out puff pastry. Bake for 25 minutes.

Turn out onto a serving dish and sprinkle with the oregano while still hot.

Sun-dried and baked tomato Tatin

Serves 6

500 g (1 lb) fresh tomatoes

2 tablespoons olive oil

2 garlic cloves, peeled and crushed

250 g (8 oz) sun-dried tomatoes in oil

1 teaspoon ground cumin

2 tablespoons olive oil

250 g (8 oz) shortcrust pastry (see page 5)

sea salt and freshly ground black pepper

rocket leaves, to garnish

Preheat the oven to its lowest setting.

Cut the fresh tomatoes into 1-cm ($^1/_2$-inch) thick slices and place on a baking sheet lined with greaseproof paper. Drizzle with olive oil and season with salt and pepper. Sprinkle the garlic over the tomatoes and bake for 20 minutes. Remove from the oven and increase the oven temperature to 200°C (400°F), gas mark 6.

Set aside 8 sun-dried tomatoes and purée the remaining sun-dried tomatoes with a little of their preserving oil and the cumin in a liquidizer or food processor, or rub through a sieve.

Arrange the reserved whole sun-dried tomatoes over the base of a baking tin, then cover with the puréed sun-dried tomato mixture.

Finally, arrange the sliced baked tomatoes over the puréed sun-dried tomato mixture and top with the rolled-out pastry. Bake for 25 minutes.

Serve garnished with the rocket leaves.

Tomato, basil and goats' cheese Tatin

Serves 6

2 x 400-g (14-oz) cans peeled whole tomatoes

1 tablespoon olive oil

3 small white onions, chopped

bunch of basil, washed and chopped

3 small, round, dried goats' cheeses

2 eggs

200 ml (7 fl oz) single cream

250 g (8 oz) ready-made puff pastry

sea salt and freshly ground black pepper

rocket leaves, to garnish

Preheat the oven to 200°C (400°F), gas mark 6.

Drain, deseed and chop the tomatoes, then fry in the olive oil with the onions and basil. Cook for about 15 minutes to make a thick sauce.

Remove the rind from the cheeses. Cut one cheese into small pieces and the remaining cheeses into slices. In a bowl, beat together the eggs, cream and goats' cheese pieces. Season with salt and pepper and add the tomato sauce.

Arrange the goats' cheese slices over the lightly oiled base of a baking tin, cover with the tomato mixture and top with the rolled-out puff pastry. Bake for 25 minutes.

Serve garnished with the rocket leaves.

Grilled aubergine and pesto Tatin

Serves 6

1 kg (2 lb) aubergines

150 ml (¼ pint) olive oil

1 jar (500 g/1 lb) aubergine caviar (see note)

1 jar (approx 130 g/5½ oz) pesto

150 g (5 oz) pine nuts, toasted

250 g (8 oz) ready-made puff pastry

sea salt and freshly ground black pepper

Preheat the grill.

Cut the aubergines lengthways into thick slices. Arrange them on the grill rack, drizzle with olive oil and season with salt and pepper. Grill for 5–6 minutes on each side, brushing with olive oil as necessary and taking care that they do not burn.

Preheat the oven to 200°C (400°F), gas mark 6.

Arrange the aubergine slices over the lightly oiled base of a baking tin, with the broader ends at the centre to form a star shape. Spread with the aubergine caviar and the pesto, and scatter with the pine nuts, reserving about 25 g (1 oz).

Top with the rolled-out pastry, then bake for 25 minutes. After turning out the tatin onto a serving plate, scatter over the reserved pine nuts.

Note: Aubergine caviar is a speciality from the Provence region of France. It is available from some delicatessen stores and speciality shops.

Pear and Roquefort Tatin

Serves 6

3 firm green pears

200 g (7 oz) Roquefort cheese

3 eggs

4 tablespoons crème fraîche

250 g (8 oz) sweet pastry (see page 5)

sea salt and freshly ground black pepper

sliced red onion, to garnish

Preheat the oven to 110°C (225°F), gas mark 1/4 .

Peel and grate the pears.

Crumble the Roquefort cheese using a fork. Beat the eggs together with the crème fraîche, then add the Roquefort and grated pears. Season with salt and pepper, but go easy on the salt as Roquefort is already very salty.

Transfer the cheese and pear mixture to a baking tin and top with the rolled-out pastry.

Bake for 10 minutes, then increase heat to 180°C (350°F), gas mark 4 and bake for a further 20 minutes.

Serve garnished with the sliced red onion.

Spinach and feta cheese Tatin

Serves 6

500 g (1 lb) spinach

50 g (2 oz) butter

250 g (8 oz) feta cheese

3 tablespoons milk

few pinches of French
4-spice powder (a blend
of white pepper, nutmeg,
ginger and cloves)

2 eggs, beaten

250 g (8 oz) shortcrust
pastry (see page 5)

sea salt and freshly ground
black pepper

Pick over and wash the spinach, then fry in the butter in a frying pan until the water it produces has completely evaporated. Drain the spinach in a sieve, pressing down hard with a wooden spoon to remove all the liquid.

Preheat the oven to 180°C (350°F), gas mark 4.

Crumble the feta cheese into a bowl, add the milk, season with pepper and sprinkle over pinches of French 4-spice powder to taste. Add the eggs and stir well.

In a large mixing bowl, combine the spinach with the feta cheese mixture. Transfer to a baking tin and top with the rolled-out pastry. Bake for 25 minutes.

Peppers and tapenade Tatin

Serves 6

2 red peppers

2 green peppers

2 yellow peppers

100 g (3½ oz) black and green olives, pitted

300 g (10 oz) tapenade (olive and anchovy paste, available from delicatessen stores and some larger supermarkets)

250 g (8 oz) shortcrust pastry (see page 5)

sea salt and freshly ground black pepper

Preheat the oven to 180°C (350°F), gas mark 4.

Wash the peppers, place them on a baking sheet lined with greaseproof paper, and bake for 20 minutes, turning regularly. When they are blackened all over, seal them in a plastic bag for 10 minutes. This will make them much easier to peel. Remove the skin and seeds, then leave the peppers to drain.

Increase the oven temperature to 200°C (400°F), gas mark 6.

Cut the peppers into thin slices and crush the olives.

Combine the tapenade with the olives and season to taste.

Arrange the pepper slices evenly over the lightly oiled base of a baking tin, alternating the colours, then spread with the tapenade and olive mixture. Top with the rolled-out pastry and bake for 25 minutes.

Peppers and garlic Tatin

Serves 6

1 bag grilled and skinned
frozen peppers (see note)

250 ml (8 fl oz) olive oil

8 garlic cloves

250 g (8 oz) ready-made
puff pastry

sea salt and freshly ground
black pepper

small bunch of fresh
mixed herbs and coriander,
to garnish

Thaw the peppers according to the manufacturer's instructions on the packet and place them on a sheet of kitchen paper to drain.

In a large pan, gently heat the olive oil, add the garlic cloves, without removing the skins, and cook slowly for 15 minutes.

Preheat the oven to 200°C (400°F), gas mark 6.

Drain and peel the garlic, reserving a little of the oil, then cut each clove in half.

Arrange the pepper pieces evenly over the base of a baking tin brushed with a little of the garlic cooking oil, season with salt and pepper and tuck the garlic cloves in among the peppers. Top with the rolled-out pastry and bake for 25 minutes.

Chop the fresh mixed herbs and the coriander. Turn the tart out onto a serving dish and sprinkle with the chopped herbs.

Note: If frozen peppers are unavailable, prepare six peppers as for the Peppers and tapenade Tatin on page 46.

Artichoke and anchovy Tatin

Serves 6

2 x 280 g (9 oz) jars baby
artichokes (or about 12)
preserved in oil, drained

1 x 200 g (7 oz) can tuna
in oil

20 anchovy fillets

1 jar Italian capers (about
100 g/3½ oz), drained

250 g (8 oz) ready-made
puff pastry

Remove the artichokes from the jar and drain on a wire rack
or kitchen paper.

Preheat the oven to 200°C (400°F), gas mark 6.

Blend the tuna with its oil, 5 of the anchovy fillets and the
capers in a liquidizer or food processor.

Arrange the 15 whole anchovy fillets in a star shape on the
base of a baking tin, then place the whole artichokes
between the anchovy spokes. Spread with the tuna, caper
and anchovy paste and top with the rolled-out pastry, taking
care to seal the edges well. Bake for 25 minutes.

Onion and sultana Tatin

Serves 6

2 tablespoons olive oil

1 tablespoon argan oil (available from delicatessen stores)

1 kg (2 lb) frozen finely sliced onions

1 clove

1 teaspoon grated fresh root ginger (or ½ teaspoon ground ginger)

1 heaped tablespoon plain flour

3 tablespoons sherry vinegar

1 chicken stock cube

150 g (5 oz) sultanas

250 g (8 oz) ready-made puff pastry

sea salt and freshly ground black pepper

Heat the olive and argan oils in a large frying pan, then add the onions and clove and fry for 15 minutes until golden, stirring to ensure they do not stick. Add the ginger. Sprinkle in the flour, stir well, and then add the vinegar. Season with salt and pepper and cook for a further 10 minutes.

Preheat the oven to 200°C (400°F), gas mark 6.

Dissolve the chicken stock cube in 500 ml (17 fl oz) boiling water. Soak the sultanas in the stock for 20 minutes. Strain, discard the stock and mix the sultanas into the onions.

Spread the onion and sultana mixture over the base of a baking tin. Top with the rolled-out pastry and bake for 25 minutes.

Delicious served with blue cheese.

Fig and pancetta Tatin

Serves 6

8 slices of pancetta

6 fresh figs

2 tablespoons olive oil

4 tablespoons balsamic vinegar

250 g (8 oz) ready-made puff pastry

freshly ground black pepper

In a non-stick frying pan, brown the pancetta slices on both sides, without adding any oil – it will produce enough fat of its own. Drain on a sheet of kitchen paper.

Preheat the oven to 200°C (400°F), gas mark 6.

Starting from the stalk end, cut the figs in half. Heat the oil in a frying pan, brown the figs for 2 minutes on each side, then remove. Deglaze the pan with the balsamic vinegar, then reduce until the juices caramelize.

Pour the caramelized juices over the base of a baking tin, arrange the figs, cut sides down, evenly over the base, season with pepper, then cover with the pancetta slices. Top with the rolled-out pastry, taking care to seal it firmly to the sides of the baking tin, and bake for 25 minutes.

Courgette and mint Tatin

Serves 6

1 kg (2 lb) small courgettes

2 tablespoons olive oil

bunch of mint

2 x 400-g (14-oz) cans chopped tomatoes, boiled until reduced in quantity by half

3 eggs, beaten

250 g (8 oz) ready-made puff pastry

sea salt and freshly ground black pepper

Trim the courgettes, cut them into quarters lengthways, removing any seeds, then cut into 3 cm (1¼-inch) chunks.

Heat the oil in a frying pan, then quickly fry the courgettes on all sides over a high heat until golden. Season with salt and pepper.

Preheat the oven to 200°C (400°F), gas mark 6.

Chop the mint, reserving a few whole leaves. In a large mixing bowl, combine the reduced tomatoes with the eggs and chopped mint and adjust the seasoning.

Arrange the courgette pieces evenly over the base of a baking tin, spread with the tomato and egg mixture and top with the rolled-out pastry. Bake for 25 minutes.

When cooked, remove the tart from the oven, turn it out onto a serving dish and garnish with the reserved whole mint leaves.

Chicory Tatin

Serves 6

1 kg (2 lb) chicory heads, blanched

100 g (3½ oz) butter

few pinches of curry powder

2 tablespoons soft brown sugar

250 g (8 oz) shortcrust pastry (see page 5)

sea salt and freshly ground black pepper

Trim the chicory, then cut across in to 2.5-cm (1-inch) pieces.

Melt 75 g (3 oz) of the butter in a frying pan and brown the chicory pieces on all sides, turning frequently and carefully, then season with salt and pepper.

Preheat the oven to 180°C (350°F), gas mark 4.

When the chicory pieces begin to soften, after about 30 minutes, sprinkle with the curry powder and boil off any remaining cooking liquid.

Sprinkle the sugar over the base of a baking tin, dot with the remaining butter, then arrange the chicory evenly, with the cut edges facing downwards. Top with the rolled-out pastry and bake for 25 minutes.

Broccoli and goats' cheese Tatin

Serves 6

3 heads of broccoli

2 spring onions

bunch of chives

300 g (10 oz) fresh goats' cheese

2 eggs

250 g (8 oz) shortcrust pastry (see page 5)

sea salt and freshly ground black pepper

Cut the broccoli heads into florets, cook for 10 minutes in salted boiling water, then remove immediately with a slotted spoon.

Preheat the oven to 180°C (350°F), gas mark 4.

Trim the spring onions and chop together with the chives.

In a large mixing bowl, beat the goats' cheese and eggs together with the spring onion and chive mixture. Season with salt and pepper.

Arrange the broccoli florets, stalk up, over the base of a baking tin. Cover with the cheese mixture, then top with the rolled-out pastry. Bake for 25 minutes.

Mushroom Tatin

Serves 6

500 g (1 lb) mixed mushrooms (e.g. oyster, cep, chanterelle, chestnut, morel, etc.)

50 g (2 oz) butter

sprig of thyme

1 tablespoon soy sauce

4 tablespoons crème fraîche

2 egg yolks

1 whole egg

pinch of grated nutmeg

pinch of curry powder

250 g (8 oz) ready-made puff pastry

sea salt and freshly ground black pepper

Trim and wipe, but do not wash, the mushrooms. Chop them into even-sized pieces, but not too finely.

Melt the butter in a large frying pan, add the mushrooms and leaves from the thyme sprig. Fry gently until brown.

Preheat the oven to 200°C (400°F), gas mark 6.

When the mushroom liquid has evaporated, add the soy sauce and stir well.

In a bowl, beat the crème fraîche with the egg yolks and whole egg. Add the nutmeg and curry powder. Season with salt and pepper and stir well.

Spread the mushrooms over the buttered base of a baking tin and cover with the crème fraîche mixture. Top with the rolled-out pastry, tucking the edges in securely towards the base of the tin. Bake for 25 minutes.

Recipe texts: Catherine Quévremont
Copy-editor: Véronique Dussidour
Recipe production: Joss Herd and Susie Theodorou
Photographs: Deirdre Rooney

© Marabout 2003
This edition published in 2004 by Hachette Illustrated UK, Octopus Publishing Group Ltd.,
2–4 Heron Quays, London E14 4JP

English translation by JMS Books LLP (email: moseleystrachan@blueyonder.co.uk)
Translation © Octopus Publishing Group Ltd.

A CIP catalogue for this book is available from the British Library

ISBN: 1 84430 097 8

Printed by Tien Wah, Singapore